# MEMORY VERSE MOT

## by Cheryl Price

### illustrated by
### Veronica Terrill

Cover by Kathy Hyndman

Shining Star Publications, Copyright © 1990
A Division of Good Apple, Inc.

ISBN No. 086653-550-0

Standardized Subject Code TA ac

Printing No. 987

**Shining Star Publications**
**A Division of Good Apple, Inc.**
**1204 Buchanan St., Box 299**
**Carthage, IL 62321-0299**

Unless otherwise indicated, the New International Version of the Bible was used in preparing the activities in this book.

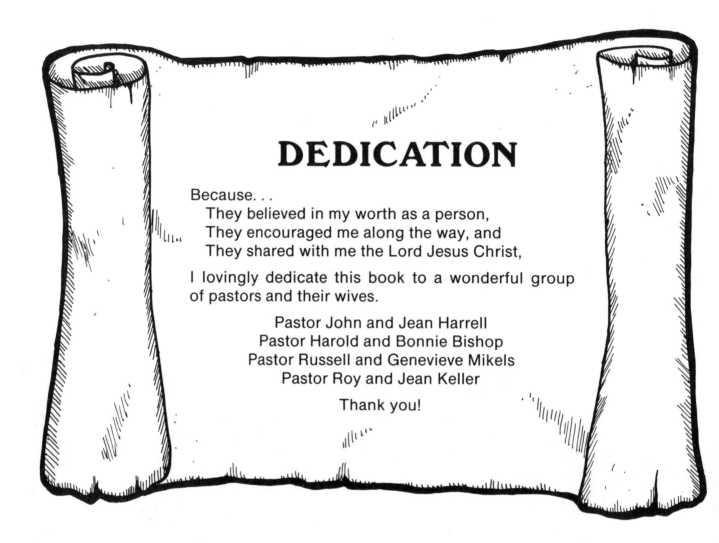

# DEDICATION

Because. . .
 They believed in my worth as a person,
 They encouraged me along the way, and
 They shared with me the Lord Jesus Christ,

I lovingly dedicate this book to a wonderful group of pastors and their wives.

Pastor John and Jean Harrell
Pastor Harold and Bonnie Bishop
Pastor Russell and Genevieve Mikels
Pastor Roy and Jean Keller

Thank you!

SS1823

# TABLE OF CONTENTS

Shining Star Publications, Copyright © 1990, A division of Good Apple, Inc.

SS1823

# NOTES FOR THE TEACHER

The activity pages in this book are reproducible. You may make a copy for each child in your classroom. . .plus one.

Plus one? Yes, it is a good idea for you to work through each project first. Make a sample of each project before you try it with your class. This will answer your questions as to the how-to of each project, and it will make you aware of the supplies you will need to complete each activity. Also, it will give the children a guide to the finished piece of work.

Don't be limited to the ideas given on these pages. Add your own touches. Use stickers, chalk, glitter, paints, etc., to make the activities more interesting. Glue sand, twigs, cotton, or blades of grass to pictures, when appropriate.

Encourage the children as they work on the memory verses and the activities. When a child is pleased with his or her work, he will take it home and share it with his family and friends. He will be sharing the Word of God and displaying it in a place of honor, where he will see it often, read it often, and hide it in his heart.

If the verses you wish to study are not represented on these pages, find an activity idea, cover the words, and copy the pattern. Type the verse you need in place of the verse in the book. Use this book as a springboard to create your own ideas.

Pray for your students: that God's Word will become real to them, and that their hearts and their minds will be open to learning His word. I pray the same for you. Bless you as you teach.

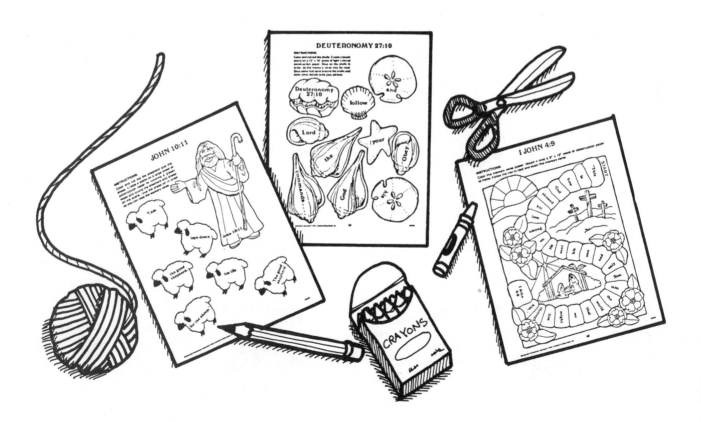

# RECORD KEEPING
## LEARNING MEMORY VERSES IS GOOD "TRAINING."

**INSTRUCTIONS:**

Copy one engine and several cars for each child. Have the children color and cut them out. Write the child's name on his/her engine. Write the reference on the train cars for each verse the child has learned. Add a new train car for each verse learned. Use this train to review the memory verses each child has learned.

(See award on page 9.)

SS1823

# RECORD KEEPING
## WATCH US GROW!

**INSTRUCTIONS:**

Make copies or enlarge the head and body of the ostrich for each member of your group. Let children color, decorate and cut out his/her own ostrich. Display each ostrich with name of appropriate student. Cut out many rectangular neck sections. Each time a child memorizes a Bible verse, he/she may add another section of neck between head and body. (List the book, chapter and verse on the neck sections.) Watch the ostriches grow as the children S-T-R-E-T-C-H their ability to memorize! Can the birds reach the ceiling in one semester? One year?

(See award on page 9.)

". . .when she spreads her feathers to run, she laughs at horse and rider."      Job 39:18

SS1823

# RECORD KEEPING
## KITE AND TAIL

**INSTRUCTIONS:**

Have each child color and cut out a kite and tail. Attach a piece of string to the back of each kite and glue the tails on at the square. Display the kites on the classroom wall or bulletin board. Each time the child learns a memory verse, write the reference on his/her kite tail.

(See award on page 10.)

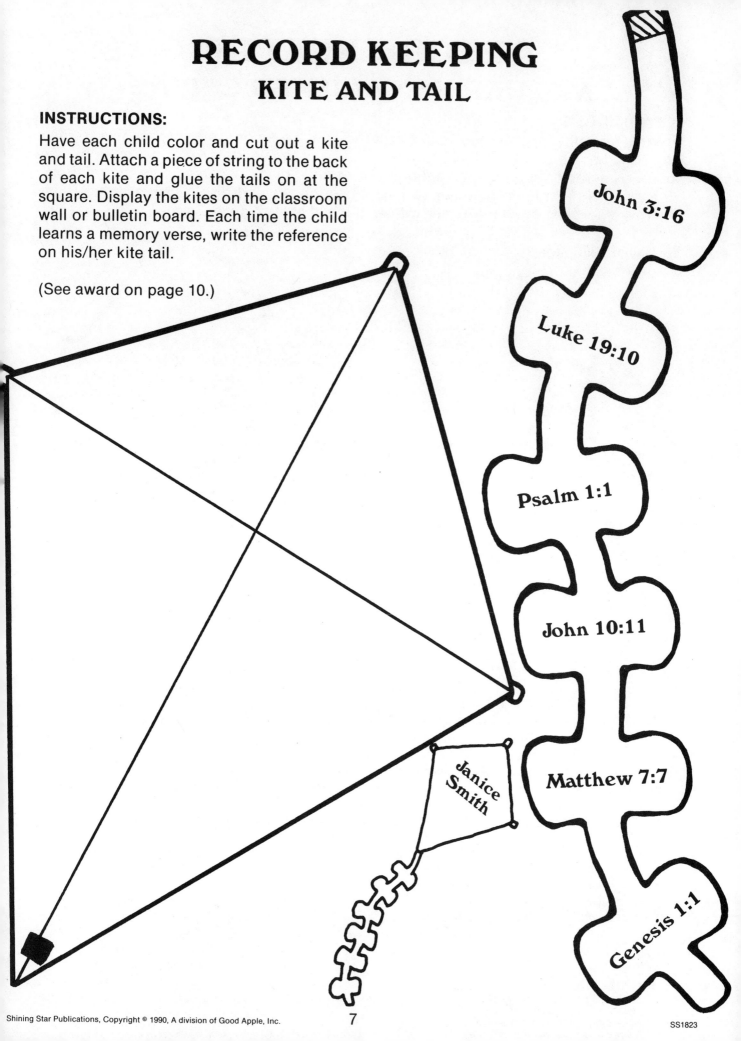

John 3:16

Luke 19:10

Psalm 1:1

John 10:11

Janice Smith

Matthew 7:7

Genesis 1:1

SS1823

# RECORD KEEPING
## MOTHER HEN AND HER CHICKS

**INSTRUCTIONS:**
Use this hen and her chicks to keep a record of each memory verse a child has learned. Copy one hen and several chicks for each child. Let the children color them. Write each child's name on a hen. Each time that child learns a memory verse, write the reference on a chick. Attach them together as the sample shows and display them in the room. Use this record to review the verses with each child at least once a month.

(See award on page 10.)

Example

SS1823

# Look who's on the right track.

_____

has done a toot-toot-terrific job learning Memory Verses.

"Train a child in the way he should go, and when he is old he will not turn from it."                    Proverbs 22:6

# Congratulations!

_____

has S-T-R-E-T-C-H-E-D

by

learning _____

New Memory Verses.

_____    _____
Presented by              Date

SS1823

Since learning _____

New Memory Verses,

_____

is

**Flying High for JESUS!**

_____ is no Chicken!

_____ has learned _____

**New Memory Verses.**

# Su...Purr Job

_____ has said
Name

_____
Memory Verse

## Purr.....fectly!

_____  _____
Presented by                        Date

# Buzzing with Good News

You will "bee" pleased to know that

_____ has learned
Name

_____.
Reference

SS1823

# GENESIS 1:1

**INSTRUCTIONS:**

God created the world in seven days. There are seven loops to this paper chain memory verse. The edges of the loops say "Day 1" to "Day 7." Draw pictures of what God created that day on each of the loops. Cut them out and glue them together in day and verse order to form a paper chain.

| glue | Genesis 1:1 | Day 7 |

| glue | "In the | Day 6 |

| glue | beginning | Day 5 |

| glue | God created | Day 4 |

| glue | the heavens | Day 3 |

| glue | and | Day 2 |

| glue | the earth." | Day 1 |

SS1823

# DEUTERONOMY 4:39

**INSTRUCTIONS:**

Color and cut out the earth and stars. Create a scene on a 12" x 18" piece of dark colored construction paper. Glue the earth at the bottom and the stars in order at the top, so you can read the memory verse.

There is

is God

in heaven

on the earth

below.

above and

no other."

"...the Lord

Deuteronomy 4:39

SS1823

# DEUTERONOMY 27:10

**INSTRUCTIONS:**

Color and cut out the shells. Create a beach scene on a 12" x 18" piece of light-colored construction paper. Glue on the shells in order, so the memory verse may be read. Glue some real sand around the shells and color other details onto your picture.

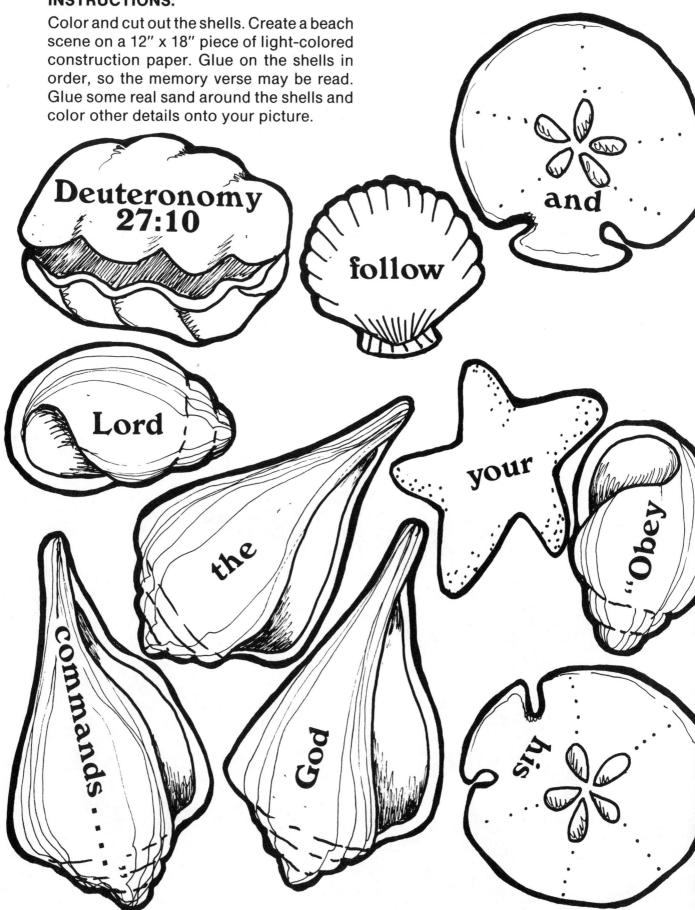

# JOSHUA 24:15

**INSTRUCTIONS:**

Color and cut out this log home and the extra logs. Mount the home on a 9" x 12" piece of construction paper. Glue the logs onto the side of the house, in order, so you can read this memory verse. Add other details to your picture if you wish.

**But as for me and my household,**

**whom you will serve, . . .**

**we will serve the Lord."**

**". . .choose for yourselves this day**

JOSHUA 24:15

SS1823

# PSALM 1:1-6

**INSTRUCTIONS:**

Color and cut out the trees and the cloud. Create a scene on a 12" x 18" sheet of construction paper. Draw a stream and some grass and sky. Place the cloud in the sky and line the trees in order so you can read these memory Scriptures in order.

Psalm 1:1-6

He is like a tree planted by streams of water, which yields its fruit in season and whose leaf does not wither. Whatever he does prospers.

Not so the wicked! They are like chaff that the wind blows away.

Therefore the wicked will not stand in the judgment, nor sinners in the assembly of the righteous.

"Blessed is the man who does not walk in the counsel of the wicked or stand in the way of sinners or sit in the seat of mockers.

For the Lord watches over the way of the righteous, but the way of the wicked will perish."

But his delight is in the law of the Lord, and on his law he meditates day and night.

16

SS1823

# PSALM 19:14

**INSTRUCTIONS:**

Color this prayer poster. Glue it to a piece of construction paper to make it more durable. Punch holes in the top where indicated. Hang this poster in a special place with a piece of yarn.

SS1823

# PSALM 56:3
## FEAR PLAQUE

**INSTRUCTIONS:**

Color and cut out the letters. Glue them onto a 8½" x 11" piece of construction paper. Glue that sheet onto a 10½" x 13" piece of contrasting color construction paper to provide a frame. Put this plaque in a special place at home to help you to remember to trust in God when you are afraid.

SS1823

# PSALM 62:8

Make a clock to help you to remember to trust in the Lord at all times.

## INSTRUCTIONS:

Color and cut out the clock and the hands. Glue the circle onto a paper plate or a 9" x 12" piece of construction paper. Hook the hands onto the clock with a metal brad.

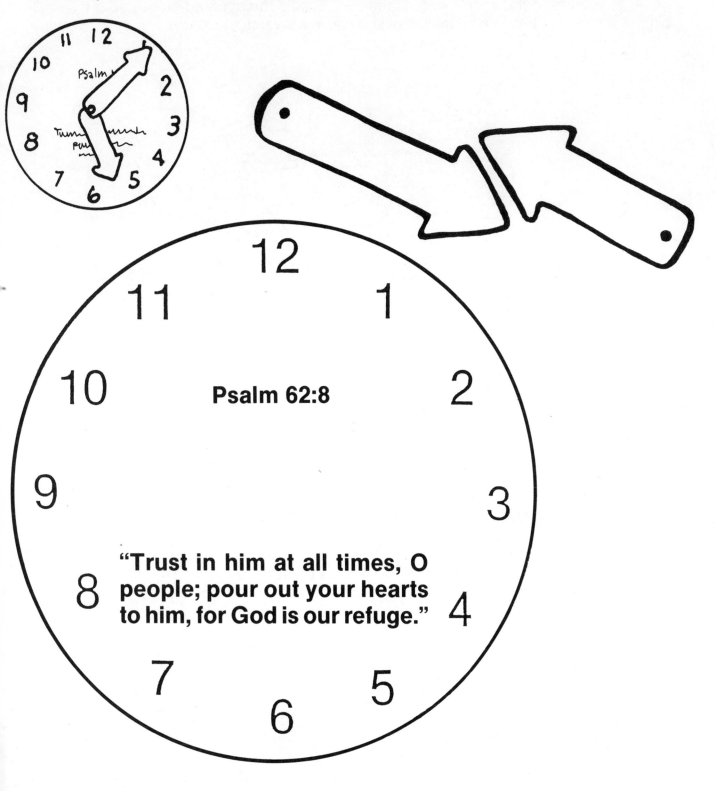

**Psalm 62:8**

**"Trust in him at all times, O people; pour out your hearts to him, for God is our refuge."**

SS1823

# PSALM 89:1

**INSTRUCTIONS:**

Paint or color a design on the back side of two paper plates. Color and cut out the memory verse circle, below, and glue it to the center on the back side of one of the plates. Staple the plates together, around the edges, leaving an opening to place 10 to 15 kernels of unpopped popcorn inside the paper plates. You may wish to staple paper streamers to the instrument as pictured. Staple the opening closed so the kernels cannot fall out. Enjoy making music as you learn this verse of praise.

**Psalm 89:1**
**"I will sing of the Lord's great love forever; with my mouth I will make your faithfulness known through all generations."**

SS1823

# PSALM 100:1-5

**INSTRUCTIONS:**

Color and cut out the train. Tape together 2-12" x 18" sheets of construction paper. Draw some grass and the sky on the construction paper. Glue the train cars on in order, so you can read and study these memory Scriptures. Add other details to your picture.

Praise

"Shout for joy to the Lord, all the earth.

Enter his gates with thanksgiving and his courts with praise; give thanks to him and praise his name.

Worship the Lord with gladness; come before him with joyful songs.

Psalm 100:1-5

For the Lord is good and his love endures forever; his faithfulness continues through all generations."

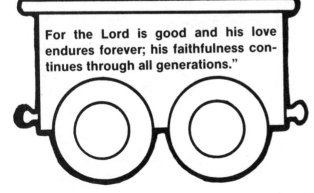

Know that the Lord is God. It is he who made us, and we are his; we are his people, the sheep of his pasture.

SS1823

# PSALM 104:24

**INSTRUCTIONS:**

Color and cut out the bird. Attach it to the tree limb with a brad. Color the rest of this memory verse poster. Frame it on a piece of 9″ x 12″ construction paper if you wish.

cut here

"How many are your works, O Lord! In wisdom you made them all; the earth is full of your creatures."

Shining Star Publications, Copyright © 1990, A division of Good Apple, Inc. SS1823

# PSALM 117

Shining Star Publications, Copyright © 1990, A division of Good Apple, Inc.

**INSTRUCTIONS:**

Decorate and cut out both hearts. (You may wish to use glitter on the small heart.) Staple the small heart over the larger one where marked. Lift the small heart each time you wish to review this verse.

**PSALM 117**

"Praise the Lord, all you nations; extol him, all you peoples. For great is his love toward us, and the faithfulness of the Lord endures forever. Praise the Lord."

SS1823

# PSALM 118:24
## CUPCAKE FLOWERS

**INSTRUCTIONS:**
Make a flower garden of blooms on a large piece of construction paper. Use flattened 2½" cupcake papers for the flower blooms. Color and cut out the circles from this page. Glue them to the centers of the cupcake papers, in order, so you can read and study this memory verse. Color the flower stems or use green pipe cleaners.

and be glad in it."

Psalm 118:24

day the Lord

has made;

let us rejoice

"This is the

# HIDDEN SCRIPTURE

## PSALM 119:9,11

**INSTRUCTIONS:**

Cover these instructions before copying this page.

Cut out the Bible shape and glue it to a 9" x 12" piece of construction paper. Color the outside edges and the ribbon. The puzzle pieces will not cover these parts. Cut out the puzzle pieces. Glue them onto the pages of this Bible shape so you can read and study these verses.

his

By

word.

119:9,11)

word

(Psalm

heart that

way pure?

not

can a

hidden

young

according

man keep

I have

in

your

living    I    sin

might    "How    your

my

to    you."

against

# PSALM 119:34
## BLOCK PICTURE

**INSTRUCTIONS:**

Color and cut out each of the 12 blocks. Punch a hole where indicated and assemble the pieces with yarn, keeping each row even. Tie the top pieces to a small stick. Tape the yarn on the back side of the stick to keep it from slipping. Hang the picture with a piece of yarn.

"Give me understanding, and I will keep your law and obey it with all my heart."

Psalm 119:34

# PSALM 122:1

**INSTRUCTIONS:**

Color and cut out the church and the stained glass window. Mount the church onto a 9" x 12" piece of construction paper. Glue the stained glass window on as a flap to cover the verse while you are memorizing or reviewing this verse. Add other details to your picture if you wish.

Psalm 122:1

glue here

"I rejoiced with those who said to me, 'Let us go to the house of the Lord.'"

SS1823

# PSALM 136:1

**INSTRUCTIONS:**

Color and cut out the circle and the spokes. Glue the circle to the center of a 9" x 12" piece of construction paper, leaving the edges free. Slip the edges of the spokes under the circle and glue them on, in order, so you can read the memory verse. Use the pattern to cut some extra plain colored spokes from construction paper. Glue them in between the other spokes to create a sunburst effect.

1st spoke here

Psalm 136:1

Plain spoke pattern

cut 5 sets

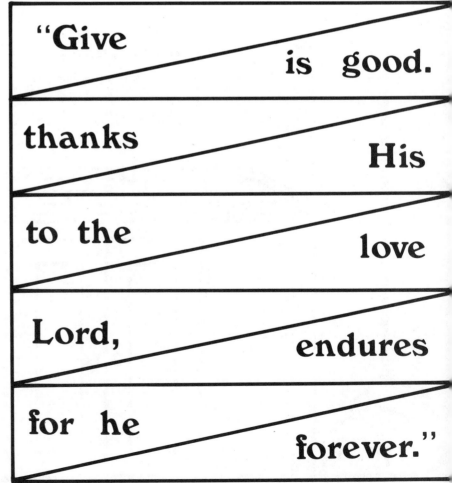

"Give    is  good.

thanks    His

to  the    love

Lord,    endures

for  he    forever."

SS182

# PSALM 143:10

**INSTRUCTIONS:**
Color and cut out the seals and the balls. Glue a seal at each end of a 12" x 18" sheet of construction paper. Glue the balls in an arch pattern between the seals. Be sure to glue the balls in order so you can read the memory verse.

 SS1823

# PSALM 145:17
## PUZZLING FISH

**INSTRUCTIONS:**

Cut out the fish shape and glue it to the top half of a 9″ x 12″ piece of construction paper. Seal a letter size envelope and tape it on three sides to the bottom half of the construction paper, to use as a pocket. Color and cut out the puzzle pieces. Place them on the fish so you can read the memory verse. Store the pieces in the envelope pocket. Rework the puzzle each time you wish to review this verse. Share your fish puzzle with your family and friends.

toward all he

145:17

and loving

has made."

Psalm

"The Lord

in all his ways

is righteous

SS182

# PSALM 150

**INSTRUCTIONS:**

Copy the praise verse, title, and plates onto heavy paper. Color them. Punch holes in each, where indicated. Stack the verses in order, and tie the booklets together with yarn or ribbon.

**A Memory Verse Booklet!**

Verses of
# PRAISE
Psalm 150

"Praise the Lord.
Praise God in his sanctuary;
praise him in his mighty heavens.

1

Praise him for his acts of power;
praise him for his surpassing greatness.

2

SS1823

# PSALM 150
## (cont'd.)

Praise him with the sounding of the trumpet, praise him with the harp and lyre,

3

praise him with tambourine and dancing, praise him with the strings and flute,

4

praise him with the clash of cymbals, praise him with resounding cymbals.

5

Let everything that has breath praise the Lord. Praise the Lord."

6

SS182

# PROVERBS 3:5-6
## TRUST

David Trusted God

Proverbs 3:5-6

SS1823

# PROVERBS 3:5-6

**INSTRUCTIONS:**

Color and cut out the memory block from this page and the memory block cover from the preceding page. Center and glue the memory block onto a 9" x 12" piece of construction paper. Cut the eight flap openings in the memory block cover on the solid lines. Carefully glue the cover over the memory block. Make sure you do not get any glue into the word squares or the flaps will not open. Open the flaps in order to read and study this memory verse.

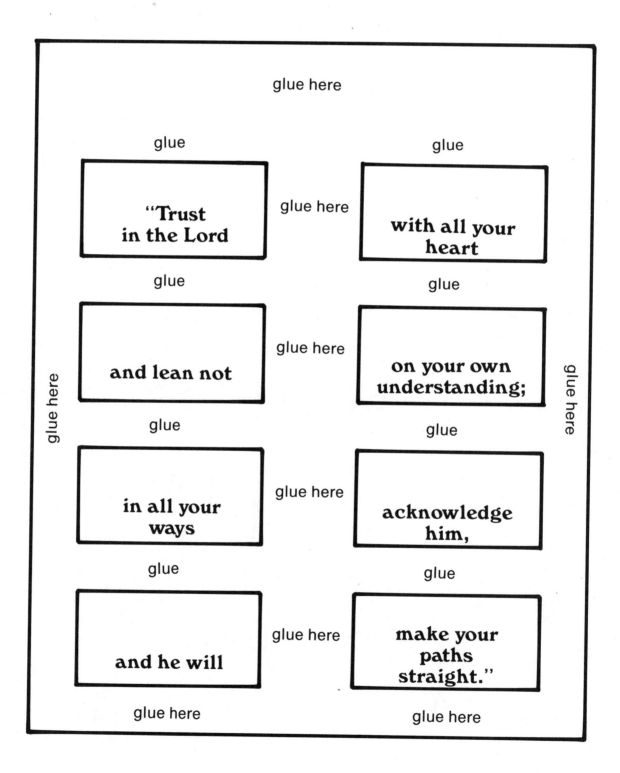

Shining Star Publications, Copyright © 1990, A division of Good Apple, Inc.                SS1823

# PROVERBS 20:11

**INSTRUCTIONS:**
Color this memory verse poster. Mount it onto a 9" x 12" piece of construction paper to frame. Follow the trail to read and study this memory verse.

Proverbs 20:11

"Even a child is known by his actions, whether by conduct his is pure and right."

# PROVERBS 22:1

**INSTRUCTIONS:**

Use pattern 2 to cut out a circle from lightweight cardboard. Cut a piece of ½" wide ribbon about 18" long. Staple the ends of the ribbon to the backside of the cardboard circle. Color and cut out the other circles and write your name on circle 3. Glue circle 1 to the front side and circle 3 to the backside of the cardboard circle. As you wear this memory verse medal, remember that you have something that is more precious than silver or gold. . .a good name.

**More valuable than Olympic Gold!**

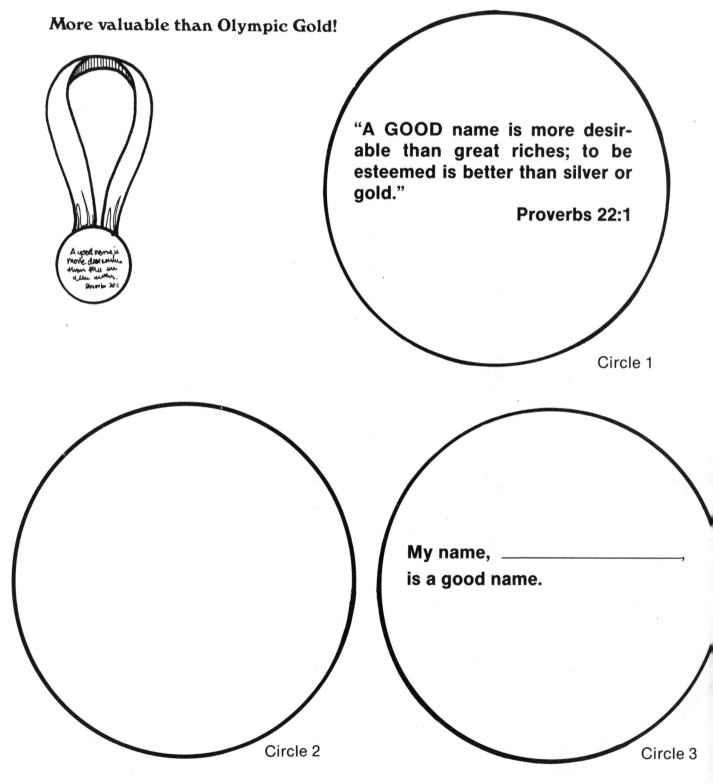

"A GOOD name is more desirable than great riches; to be esteemed is better than silver or gold."

Proverbs 22:1

Circle 1

Circle 2

My name, _____, is a good name.

Circle 3

SS182

# ISAIAH 1:18

**INSTRUCTIONS:**
Color and cut out the snowflakes. Create a snowy scene on a 12" x 18" sheet of construction paper. Glue the snowflakes on in order so you can read this memory verse. You may wish to glue cotton to the bottom of your picture to show how much it has snowed.

SS1823

# NAHUM 1:7
## LAMB PUZZLE

**INSTRUCTIONS:**

Cut out the lamb shape and glue it to the top half of a 9" x 12" piece of construction paper. Seal a letter size envelope and tape it on three sides to the bottom half of the construction paper, to use as a pocket. Color and cut out the puzzle pieces. Place them on the lamb so you can read the memory verse. Store the pieces in the envelope pocket. Rework the puzzle each time you wish to review this verse. Share this verse puzzle with your family and friends.

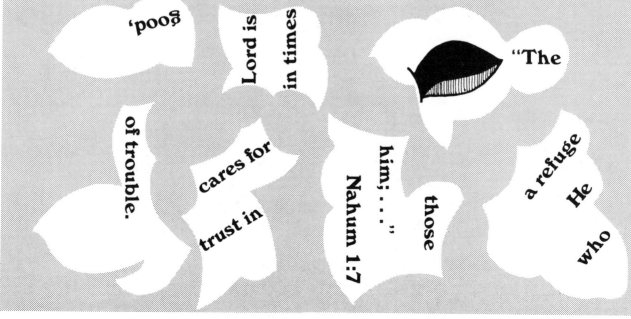

 SS1823

# MALACHI 3:10

**INSTRUCTIONS:**

Color and cut out the pumpkins and the corn stalk. On a large sheet of construction paper, glue the pumpkins on in order so you can read the verse. Add other details to your picture.

and pour out so much blessing

Test me in this," says the Lord Almighty,

that there may be food in my house.

that you will not have room enough for it."

Malachi 3:10

"Bring the whole tithe into the storehouse,

"and see if I will not throw open the flood gates of heaven

SS1823

# MATTHEW 5:3-10

In a very special message, Jesus told his followers about the true blessings of this life. We call that message, "The Sermon on the Mount." It begins with the Beatitudes which are found in Matthew 5:3-10.

Read and talk about the Beatitudes with your students. Make sure the students understand the meanings of any difficult words.

Give each student a copy of the Beatitudes puzzle, found on the next three pages. Have them color the suns and the rainbows. Leave the clouds white. Color and cut out the activity instruction square and glue it to the front of a legal size (4⅛" x 9½") envelope. Laminate and cut out all the review pieces.

Review these verses by matching the correct rainbows and clouds. Store the review pieces in the envelopes.
Example

**INSTRUCTIONS:**
Study the teachings of Jesus in Matthew 5:3-10.

 Match the rainbows and clouds together. Read the Scripture again to see how many you have matched correctly.

Activity Instruction Square

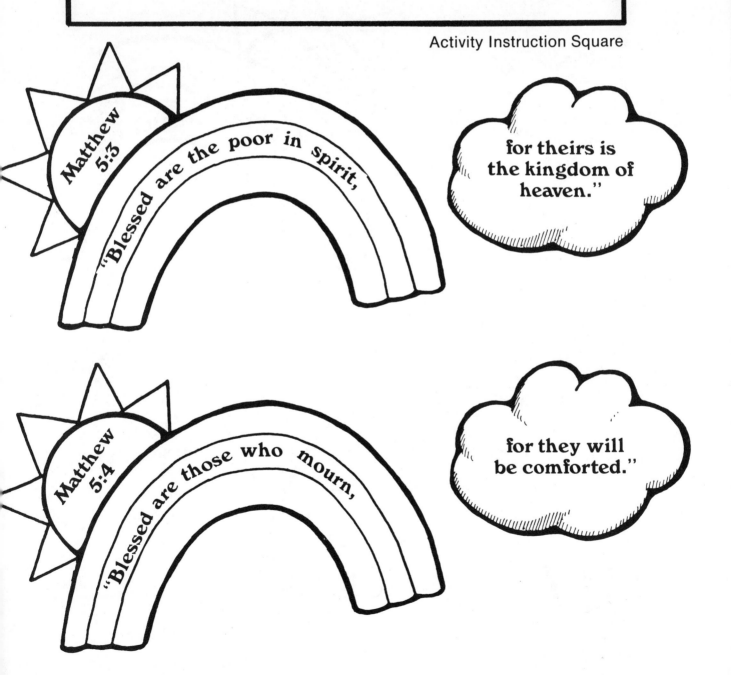

Matthew 5:3 "Blessed are the poor in spirit,

for theirs is the kingdom of heaven."

Matthew 5:4 "Blessed are those who mourn,

for they will be comforted."

 SS1823

Matthew 5:5

"Blessed are the meek,

for they will inherit the earth."

for they will be filled."

Matthew 5:6

"Blessed are those who hunger and thirst for righteousness,

Matthew 5:7

"Blessed are the merciful,

for they will be shown mercy."

SS1823

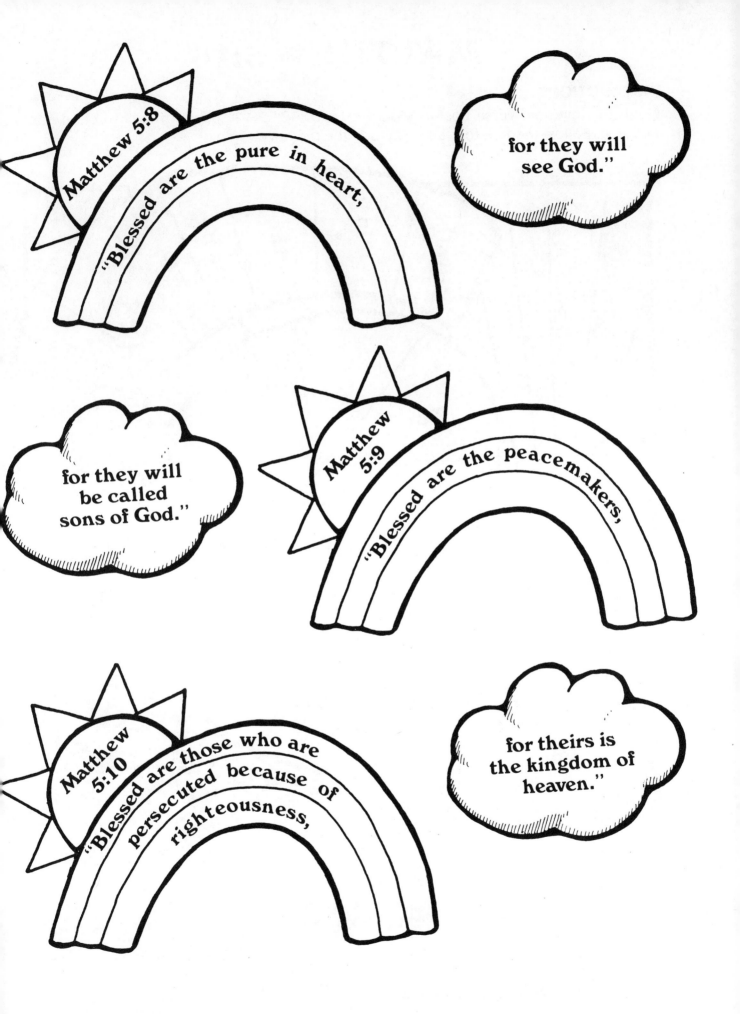

Matthew 5:8

"Blessed are the pure in heart,

for they will see God."

for they will be called sons of God."

Matthew 5:9

"Blessed are the peacemakers,

Matthew 5:10

"Blessed are those who are persecuted because of righteousness,

for theirs is the kingdom of heaven."

SS1823

# MATTHEW 5:16

**INSTRUCTIONS:**

Color this memory verse poster. Mount it onto a 9" x 12" piece of construction paper to frame. Follow the trail to read and study the memory verse.

SS1823

# MATTHEW 6:9-13
## THE LORD'S PRAYER

**INSTRUCTIONS:**

Cut out the praying hands and the reference. Punch holes at the X's and loop the pieces together to form a chain. Hang the chain where it will remind you to pray every day.

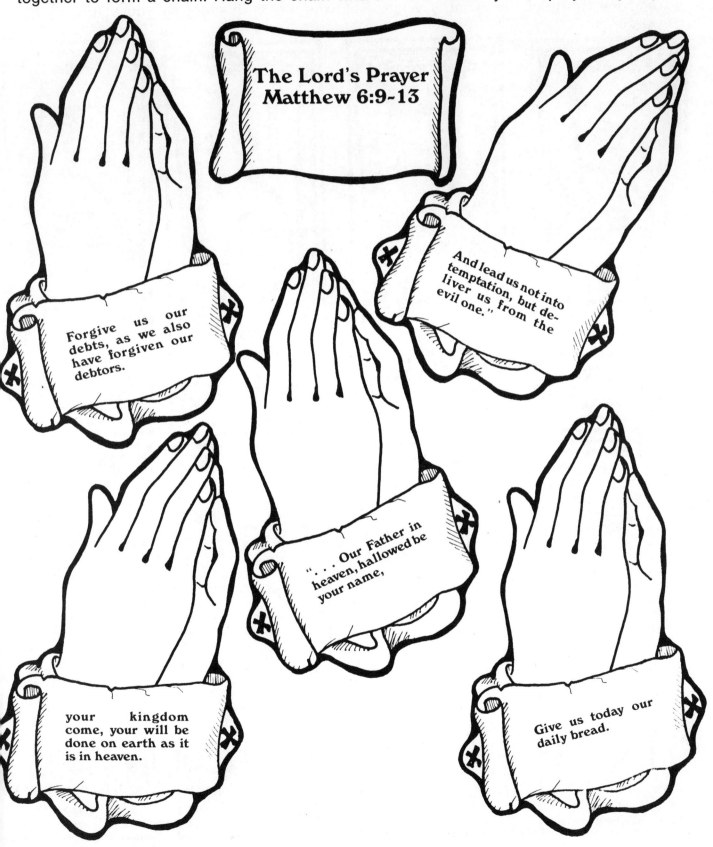

The Lord's Prayer
Matthew 6:9-13

And lead us not into temptation, but deliver us from the evil one."

Forgive us our debts, as we also have forgiven our debtors.

". . . Our Father in heaven, hallowed be your name,

your kingdom come, your will be done on earth as it is in heaven.

Give us today our daily bread.

SS1823

# MATTHEW 6:24
## COUNTING THE COST

**INSTRUCTIONS:**

Color each bill green, then cut it out. Highlight the words of the memory verse with a yellow marker. Act like you are counting the money, but as you lay each bill down, read the words of the memory verse. Read the words in order so you can learn this verse.

SS182

# MATTHEW 6:31-33

**INSTRUCTIONS:**
Color and cut out the "Ladder of Success" piece and each step. Punch a hole at each X. Use yarn to loop each step together in order.

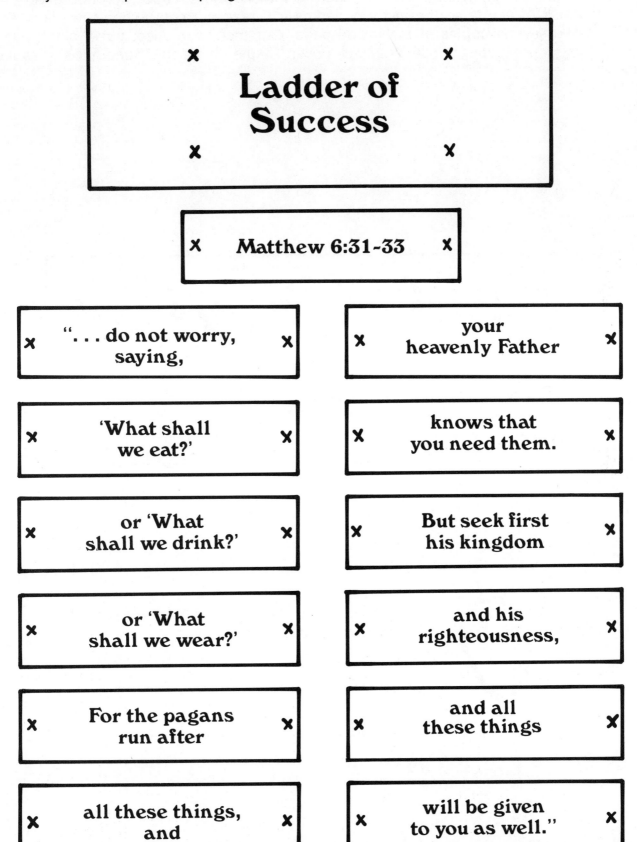

Ladder of Success

x Matthew 6:31-33 x

x "... do not worry, saying, x    x your heavenly Father x

x 'What shall we eat?' x    x knows that you need them. x

x or 'What shall we drink?' x    x But seek first his kingdom x

x or 'What shall we wear?' x    x and his righteousness, x

x For the pagans run after x    x and all these things x

x all these things, and x    x will be given to you as well." x

    SS1823

# MATTHEW 7:7-8
## MY PRAYER RECORD

**INSTRUCTIONS:**

Color and cut out the front cover and each of the six doors. Glue each door over the correct block of words so the memory verses will read correctly when the doors are lifted. Make several copies of the inside page. Cut them out. Also, cut a blank page from construction paper to use as a back cover. Staple the booklet together across the top.

Inside page

_____

Date

**My Prayer Record**

_____

_____

_____

_____

_____

**Note below. . .the date and how this prayer was answered**

_____

_____

_____

SS1823

# MATTHEW 7:7-8

## MY PRAYER RECORD
## MATTHEW 7:7-8

| glue | glue | glue |
|------|------|------|
| and it will be given to you; | and you will find; | and the door will be opened to you. |

| glue | glue | glue |
|------|------|------|
| receives; | finds; | the door will be opened." |

| | | |
|------|------|------|
| "Ask | Seek | Knock |

| | | |
|------|------|------|
| For everyone who asks | he who seeks | and to him who knocks, |

# MATTHEW 7:12

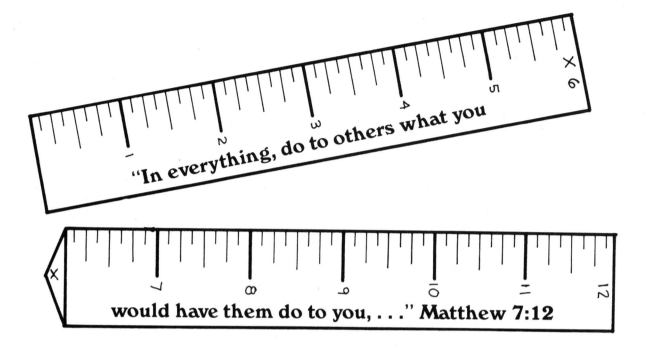

"In everything, do to others what you would have them do to you, . . ." Matthew 7:12

**INSTRUCTIONS:**

Color the ruler and laminate or mount onto lightweight cardboard. Cut it out. Match the X's and hook the two pieces together with a brad. Remember this "rule" in everything you do.

_____ Really

**Measures Up!**

**Congratulations
on learning Matthew 7:12**

_____
Presented by

_____
Date

". . .With the measure you use, it will be measured to you . . . ."
Mark 4:24

Shining Star Publications, Copyright © 1990, A division of Good Apple, Inc.

SS1823

# MATTHEW 11:28

**INSTRUCTIONS:**

Color both figures. Laminate them or mount them on lightweight cardboard. Cut out the figures and the window on figure A. Match the figures at the dot, and hook them together with a brad. Turn the bottom wheel to read and study the memory verse.

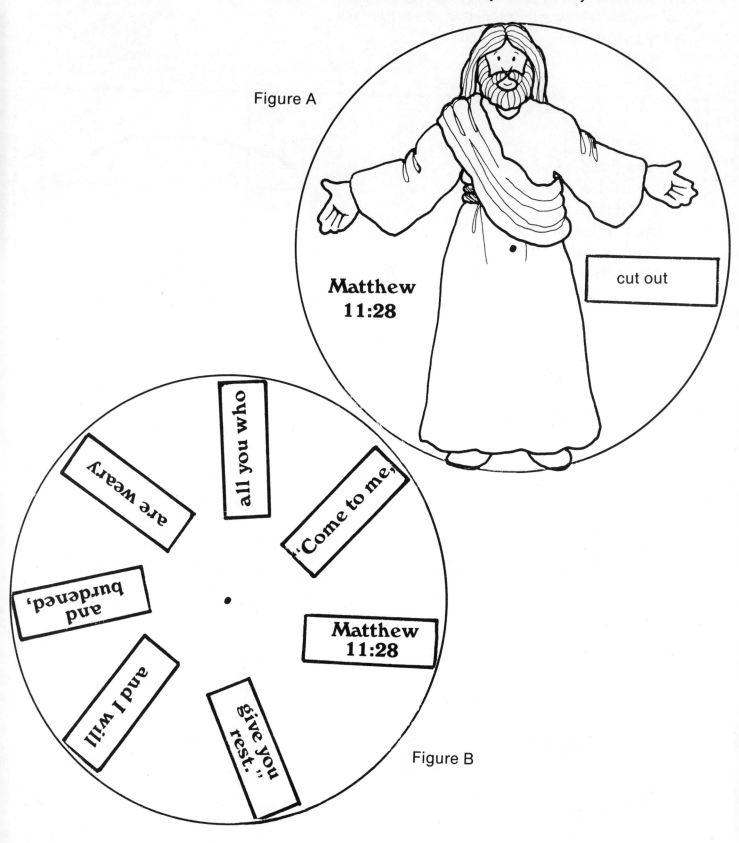

Figure A

Matthew
11:28

cut out

Figure B

SS1823

# MATTHEW 19:14
## BLOCK PICTURE

**INSTRUCTIONS:**

Cut out all twelve blocks and glue them in order, onto a 9″ x 12″ piece of construction paper. Color this memory verse poster.

"Jesus said, 'Let the little children come to me, and do not hinder them, for the kingdom of heaven belongs to such as these.'"

Matthew 19:14

SS1823

# MATTHEW 24:35

**INSTRUCTIONS:**

Color and cut out the apples. Draw a picture of a large tree on a 12" x 18" piece of construction paper. Glue the apples on the tree, in order, so you can read the verse. Add other details to the picture if you wish.

but

away,

Matthew 24:35

will

pass

and

earth

"Heaven

my

never

away."

pass

will

words

SS1823

# MARK 4:41

**INSTRUCTIONS:**

Color and cut out the windmill and the blades. Glue the windmill picture onto a 9″ x 12″ piece of construction paper. Attach the blades with a metal brad. As you turn the blades, read and study this memory verse.

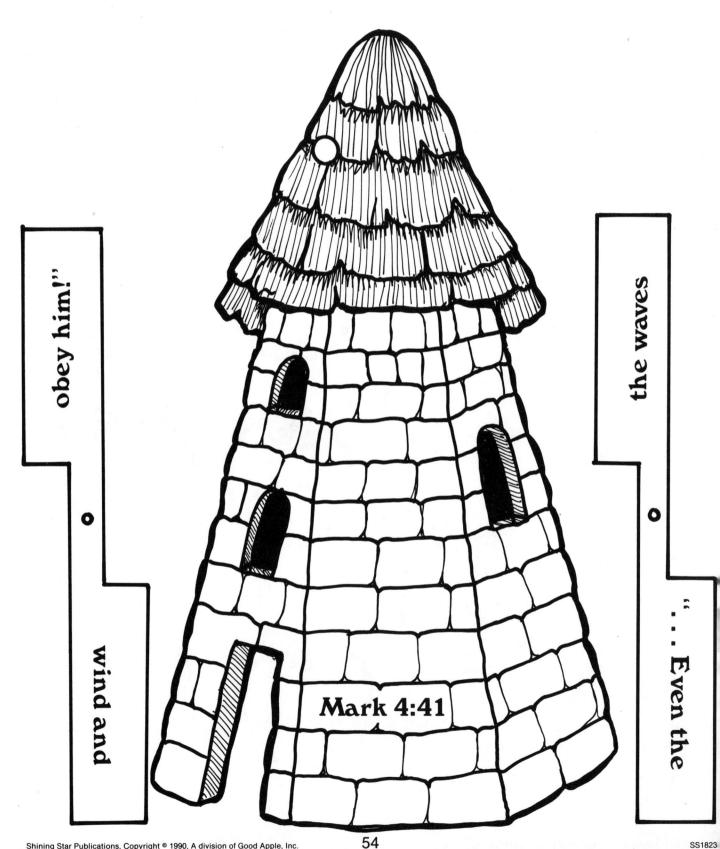

obey him!"

wind and

the waves

"... Even the

Mark 4:41

SS1823

# MARK 11:9
## PALM BRANCH MEMORY WRAP

**INSTRUCTIONS:**

Color the large palm branch. Laminate it or mount it on lightweight cardboard. Cut it out. Punch a hole where the X is at the base of the branch. Tie a one yard long piece of string or yarn through this hole. Wrap the string from notch to notch as you read each word in this memory verse.

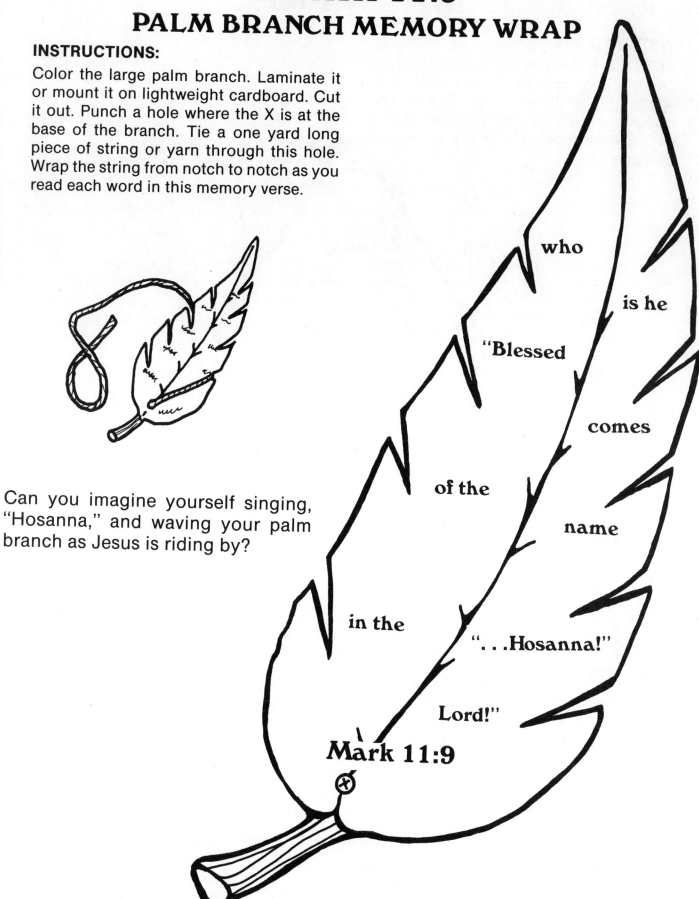

Can you imagine yourself singing, "Hosanna," and waving your palm branch as Jesus is riding by?

who

is he

"Blessed

comes

of the

name

in the

"...Hosanna!"

Lord!"

Mark 11:9

SS1823

# MARK 11:17

**INSTRUCTIONS:**

Color the church and the praying child. Laminate or mount each piece onto lightweight cardboard. Cut out and with backs together, glue churches and praying child pieces together. Hang as a mobile using yarn.

Note: Two copies of the church and two copies of the praying child will be needed for each mobile.

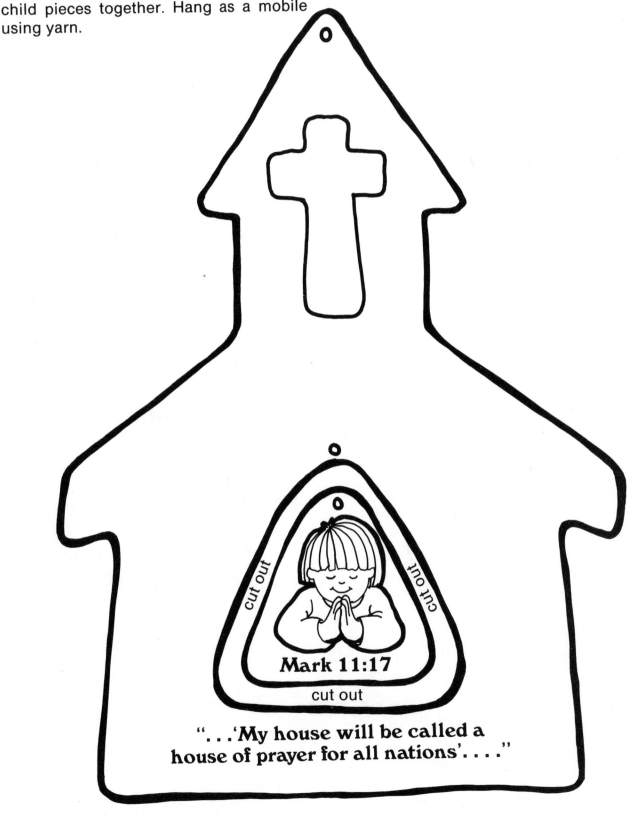

cut out

cut out

cut out

**Mark 11:17**

"...'My house will be called a
house of prayer for all nations'...."

SS1823

# MARK 16:15

**INSTRUCTIONS:**

Color both figures. Laminate them or mount them on lightweight cardboard. Cut out the figures and the window on figure A. Match the figures at the dot, and hook them together with a brad. Turn the bottom wheel to read and study the memory verse.

Figure A

cut out

North America

Greenland

Central America

Pacific Ocean

Atlantic Ocean

Africa

South America

**Mark 16:15**

Figure B

the good news

and preach

to all creation."

world

Mark 16:15

"Go into all the

He said to them.

# LUKE 6:27-28

"...Love your enemies, who hate you, to those do good bless those who curse you, pray for those who mistreat you." Luke 6:27-28

58

# LUKE 10:27

**INSTRUCTIONS:**
Color and cut out the three heart pieces. Match the hearts at the dots, with figure A on top, figure B in the middle and figure C on the bottom. Hook the pieces together with a metal brad. Open the front hearts to read and study this memory verse.

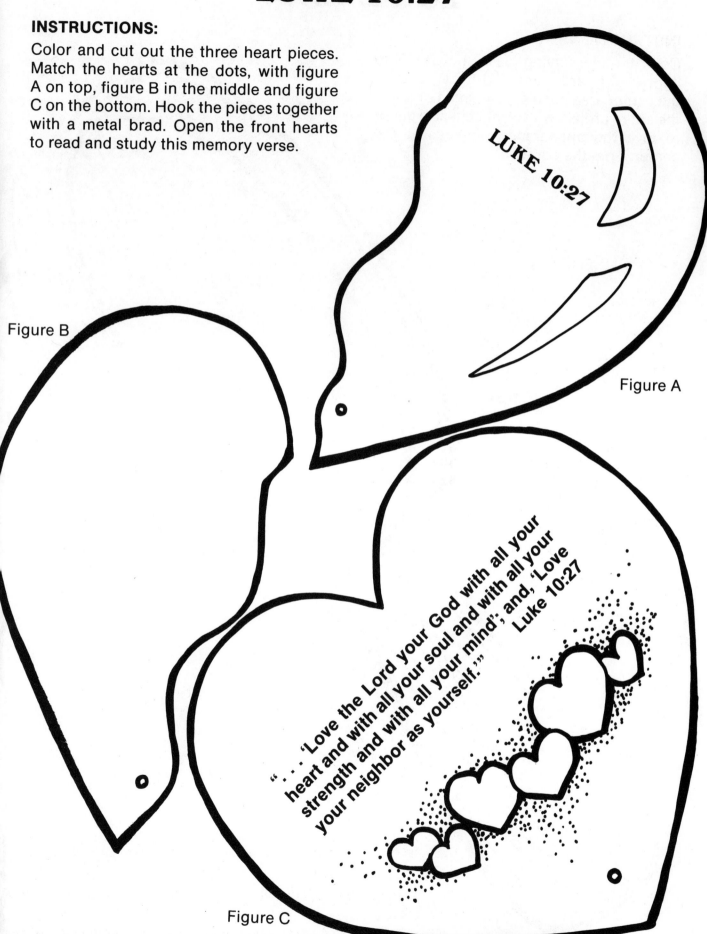

Figure B

Figure A

Figure C

"... 'Love the Lord your God with all your heart and with all your soul and with all your strength and with all your mind'; and, 'Love your neighbor as yourself.'" Luke 10:27

59

SS1823

# LUKE 19:10

**INSTRUCTIONS:**

Color the magnifying glass and glue it to lightweight cardboard. Cut it out, cutting the center area out also. Laminate or cover the entire project with clear adhesive paper to give the appearance of glass in the center. Trim the edges.

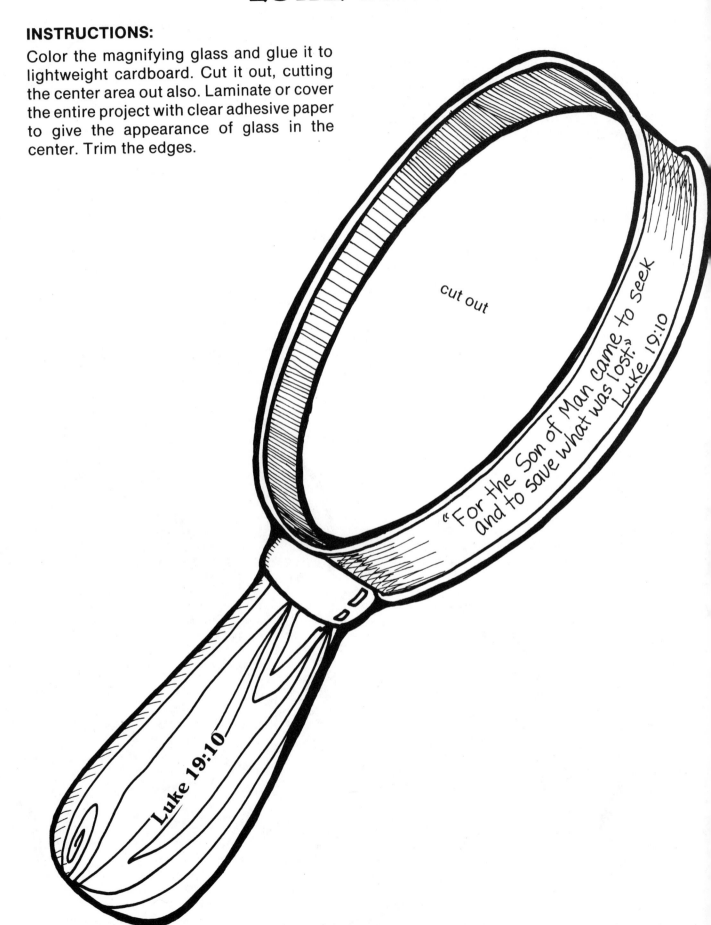

cut out

"For the Son of Man came to seek and to save what was lost." Luke 19:10

Luke 19:10

60

SS182

# LUKE 24:34
## A BOOKMARK TO COLOR AND TO KEEP

**INSTRUCTIONS:**

Color and cut out this bookmark. Use it in your Bible as you learn this great promise.

It is true! The Lord has risen!

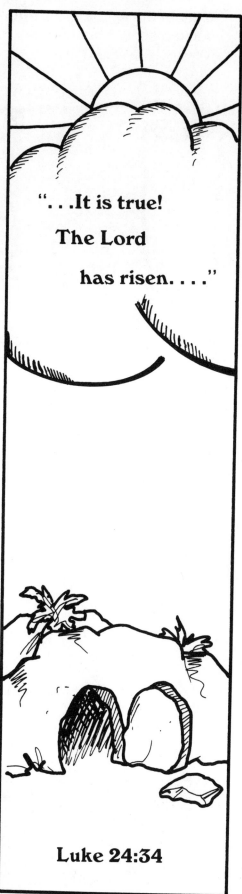

"...It is true!
The Lord
has risen. . . ."

Luke 24:34

SS1823

# JOHN 1:12

**INSTRUCTIONS:**
Cut out the words at the bottom of this page and use them to complete the above memory verse plaque. Frame it with construction paper if you wish.

"Yet to ＿＿＿＿＿＿＿＿ who

＿＿＿＿＿＿＿＿＿ him, to

those who ＿＿＿＿＿＿＿＿

in his name, he gave the

＿＿＿＿＿＿＿ to become

＿＿＿＿＿＿of God." John 1:12

**believed    all    right    children    received**

SS182

# JOHN 3:16

**INSTRUCTIONS:**

Color both figures. Laminate them or mount them on lightweight cardboard. Cut out the figures and the window on figure A. Match the figures at the dot, and hook them together with a brad. Turn the bottom wheel to read and study the memory verse.

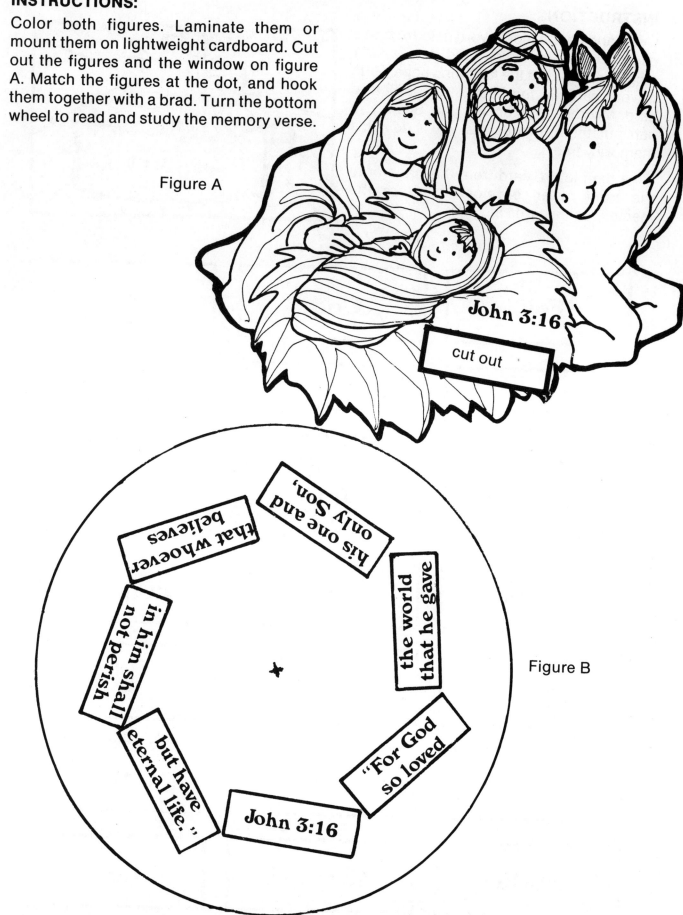

Figure A

John 3:16

cut out

Figure B

"For God so loved

the world that he gave

his one and only Son,

that whoever believes

in him shall not perish

but have eternal life."

John 3:16

SS1823

# JOHN 3:17

**INSTRUCTIONS:**

Color and cut out each word card from this page. Duplicate, color, and cut out 21 picture cards from the following page. Glue a word card on the back of each picture card. Mix the cards up in a pile. See if you can put them in order as you study this memory verse.

Glue the picture card from this page onto the front of an envelope to store the memory verse cards in.

John 3:17

| | | |
|---|---|---|
| "For | God | did |
| not | send | his |
| Son | into | the |
| world | to | condemn |
| the | world, | but |
| to | save | the |
| world | through | him." |

SS182

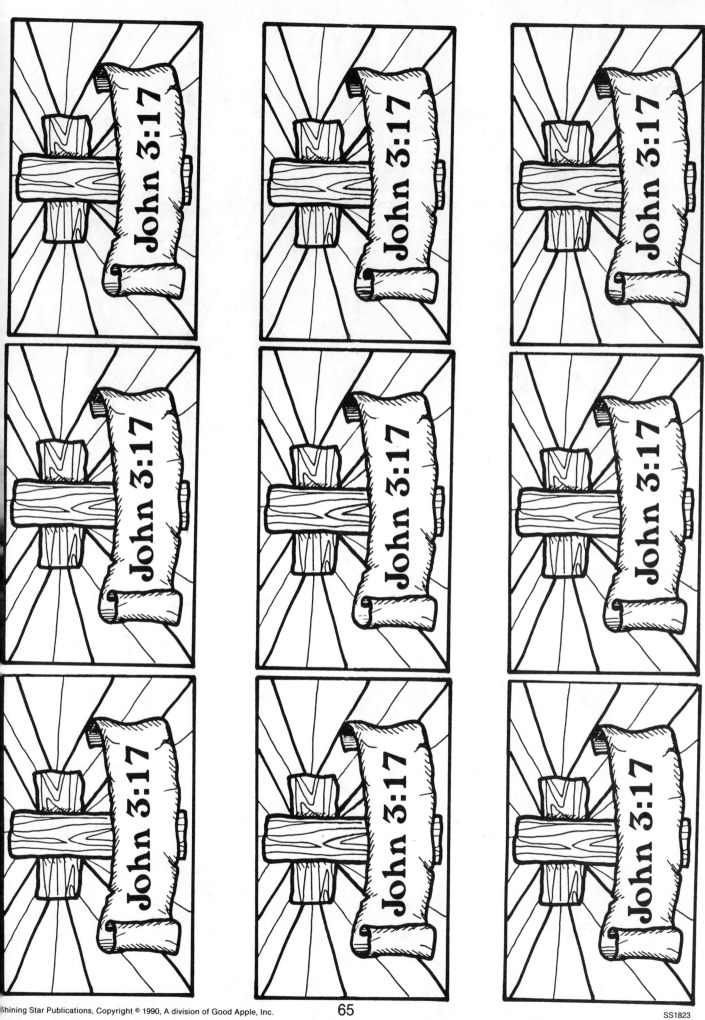

SS1823

# JOHN 10:11

**INSTRUCTIONS:**

Color and cut out the shepherd and the sheep. Create a scene on a large sheet of construction paper by coloring a grassy slope and gluing the shepherd and sheep on the scene. Glue the sheep on in order so you can read the memory verse.

"I am

lays down

John 10:11

the good shepherd.

his life

The good shepherd

for the sheep."

SS182

# JOHN 12:46

**INSTRUCTIONS:**

Color both figures. Laminate them or mount them on lightweight cardboard. Cut out the figures and the window on figure A. Match the figures at the dot, and hook them together with a brad. Turn the bottom wheel to read and study the memory verse.

Figure A

Figure B

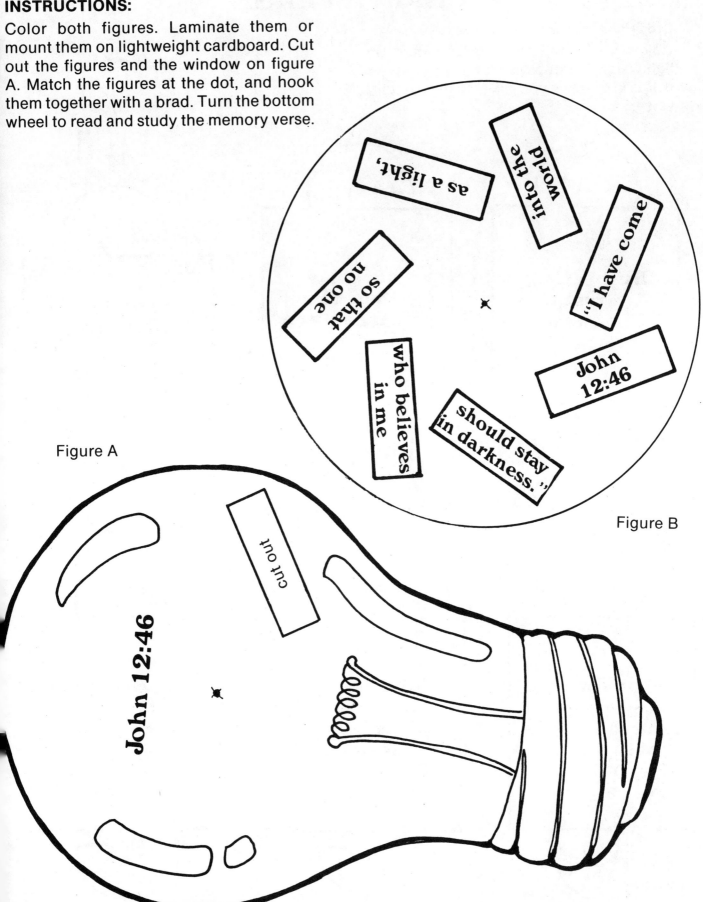

SS1823

# JOHN 14:1-3
## CHAIN A VERSE

**INSTRUCTIONS:**

Color this chain. Laminate or mount on lightweight cardboard. Cut out. Hang the words in order so you can read the memory verse.

Trust in God; trust also in me.

I am going there to prepare a place for you.

And if I go and prepare a place for you,

In my Father's house are many rooms; if it were not so, I would have told you.

John 14:1-3

"Do not let your hearts be troubled.

I will come back and take you to be with me that you also may be where I am."

SS1823

# JOHN 14:6

**INSTRUCTIONS:**
Color the chick. Cut out the egg. Fold the egg on the dotted line to cover half the chick. Open the egg to read and study this memory verse. Share this verse with your family and friends.

Look who's
Peeking Out to say. . .

Jesus is the
only way!

". . . I am the way and the truth and the life.
No one comes to the Father
except through me."
John 14:6

# JOHN 15:5

**INSTRUCTIONS:**

Color and cut out this cup wrap. Glue it around a 7" Styrofoam cup. Fill the cup with dirt and plant a small vine in it. Take the vine home. Water it once a week with only a small amount of water. Read the verse each day until you can say it without looking. Thank the Lord for His promise.

I am the vine; you are the branches. If a man remains in me and I in him, he will bear much fruit, apart from me you can do nothing

John 15:5

glue

SS182

# ACTS 1:11

**INSTRUCTIONS:**

Color the figure of Jesus and cut out all three clouds. Match the clouds, at the dots, with figure A on top, figure B in the middle and figure C on the bottom. Hook them together with a metal brad. Open the front clouds to read and study this memory verse.

". . . This same Jesus, who has been taken from you into heaven, will come back in the same way you have seen him go into heaven." Acts 1:11

C

B

A

Acts 1:11

SS1823

# ROMANS 5:8

## INSTRUCTIONS:

Color both figures. Laminate them or mount them on lightweight cardboard. Cut out the figures and the window on figure A. Match the figures at the dot, and hook them together with a brad. Turn the bottom wheel to read and study the memory verse.

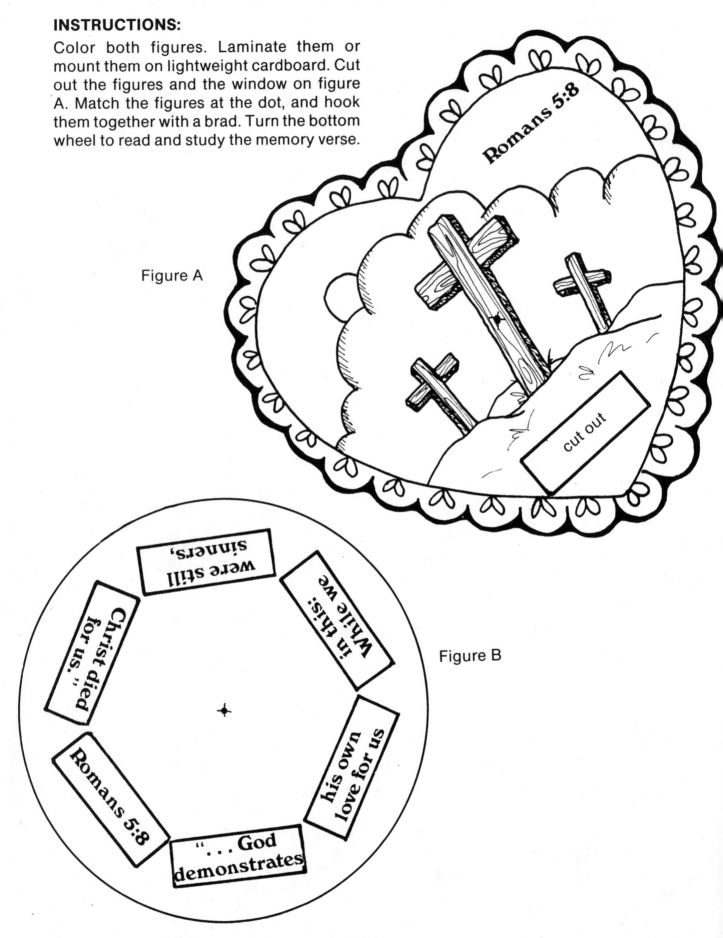

Figure A

Romans 5:8

cut out

Figure B

"...God demonstrates

Romans 5:8

Christ died for us."

were still sinners,

While we

his own love for us

in this:

SS1823

# ROMANS 6:23

**INSTRUCTIONS:**

Color and cut out this gift box. Fold the box on the dotted line toward you. Color the lid part to match the rest of the box. Cut a small slit where the dark line is. Slip a 12″ piece of yarn or ribbon through this hole and tape it to the back side of the box. Tie this ribbon into a bow to keep the gift closed until you are ready to share or review this memory verse.

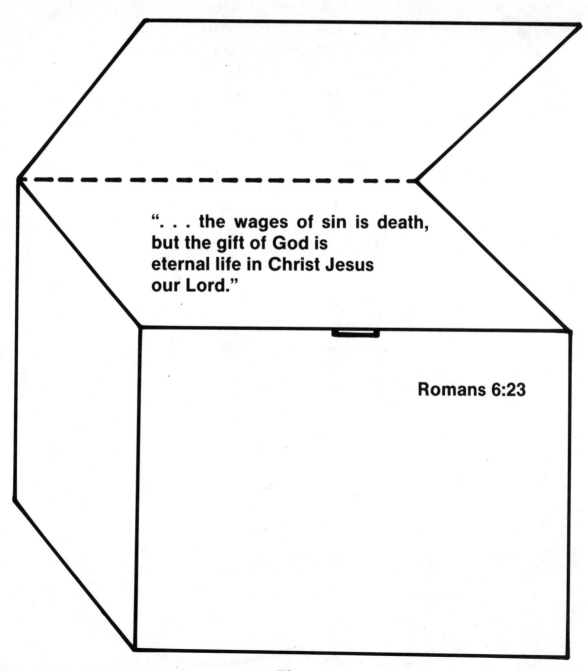

". . . the wages of sin is death, but the gift of God is eternal life in Christ Jesus our Lord."

**Romans 6:23**

SS1823

# I CORINTHIANS 10:13

**INSTRUCTIONS:**

Color and cut out two copies of this apple mobile. Glue the pieces back to back with a piece of brown yarn in the center. The pieces will not match perfectly, but this is OK. The yarn becomes the hanger for the mobile.

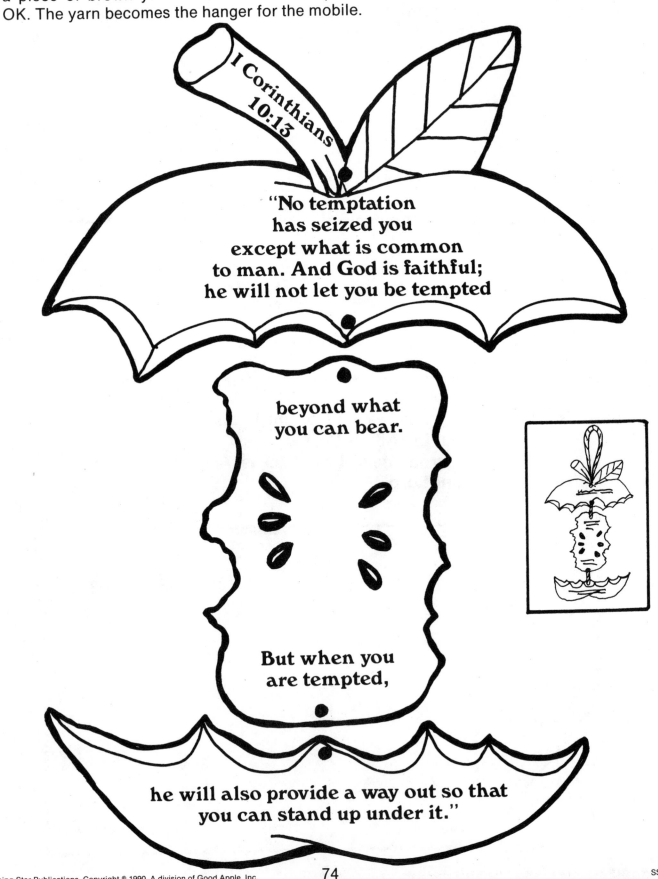

I Corinthians 10:13

"No temptation has seized you except what is common to man. And God is faithful; he will not let you be tempted

beyond what you can bear.

But when you are tempted,

he will also provide a way out so that you can stand up under it."

SS1823

# II CORINTHIANS 5:17

**INSTRUCTIONS:**
Color and cut out all four pieces. Glue the branch and cocoon onto a 9" x 12" sheet of construction paper. Glue around the edge of the cocoon and glue on the cocoon pocket. Allow the pocket to dry. Fold the butterfly in half and place it into the pocket. As you study this verse about new creatures, place the caterpillar into the cocoon and remove the butterfly and read the verse. Share this surprise butterfly with your family and friends.

II Corinthians 5:17

". . . if anyone is in Christ, he is a new creation; the old has gone, the new has come!"

II Corinthians 5:17

Glue Here

SS1823

# GALATIANS 5:22-23
## THE FRUIT OF THE SPIRIT
## MEMORY VERSE WHEEL

**INSTRUCTIONS:**

Color, laminate, cut out, and hook together with a brad.

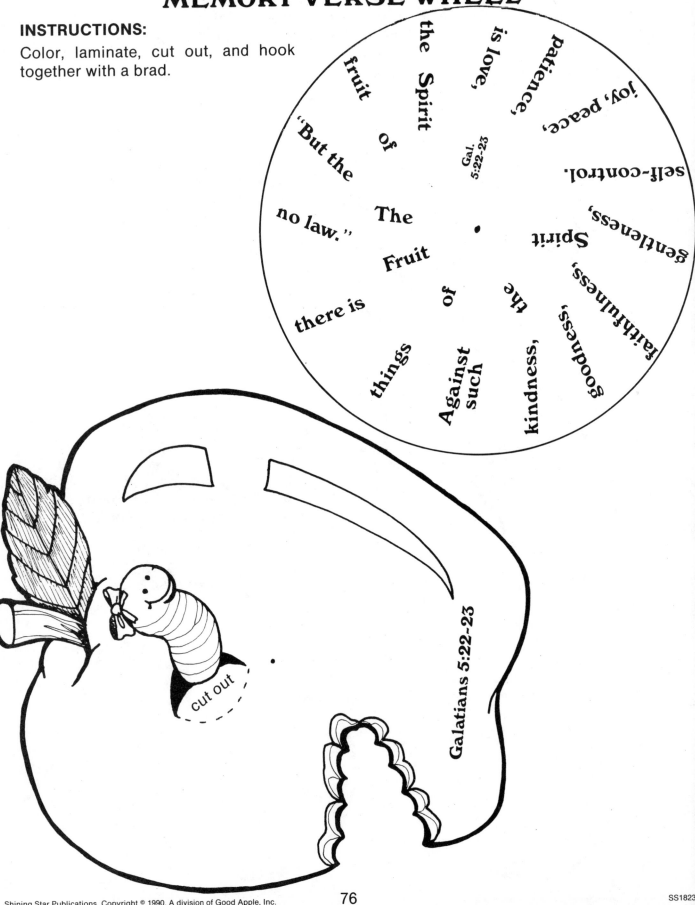

The wheel reads: "But the fruit of the Spirit is love, joy, peace, patience, kindness, goodness, faithfulness, gentleness, self-control. Against such things there is no law." The Fruit of the Spirit. Gal. 5:22-23

cut out

Galatians 5:22-23

# EPHESIANS 4:32

**INSTRUCTIONS:**
Color and cut out the bees and the hive. Create a scene on a large sheet of construction paper by gluing the bees on, in order, as they fly to the hive. Add other details to your picture.

SS1823

# EPHESIANS 6:1

**INSTRUCTIONS:**

Color and cut out the house and the door. Glue the door onto the house where indicated. Glue the house onto a large piece of construction paper. Add other details to the picture if you wish.

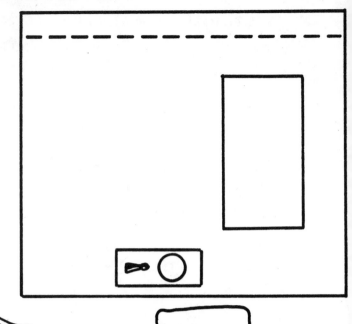

Ephesians 6:1

glue here

**"Children, obey your parents in the Lord, for this is right."**

SS1823

# PHILIPPIANS 2:14
## FIRST LETTER MOBILE

**INSTRUCTIONS:**

Color the letters. Laminate them or mount them onto lightweight cardboard and cut them out. Loop the letters together with yarn and hang them in order so you can read this memory verse.

SS1823

# COLOSSIANS 3:23
## BLOCK PICTURE

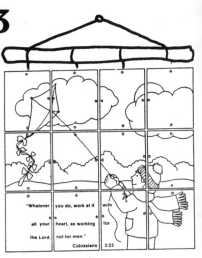

### INSTRUCTIONS:

Color and cut out each of the 12 blocks. Punch a hole where indicated and assemble the pieces with yarn, keeping each row even. Tie the top pieces to a little stick. Tape the yarn on the back side of the stick to keep it from slipping. Hang the picture with a piece of yarn.

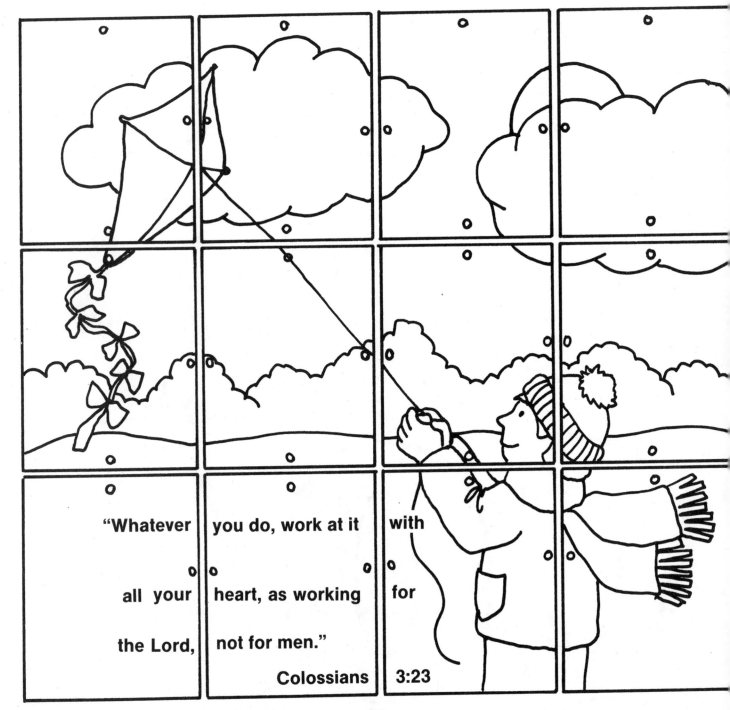

"Whatever you do, work at it with all your heart, as working for the Lord, not for men."
Colossians 3:23

Shining Star Publications, Copyright © 1990, A division of Good Apple, Inc.

SS1823

# I THESSALONIANS 5:18

**INSTRUCTIONS:**

Color both figures. Laminate them or mount them on lightweight cardboard. Cut out the figures and the window on figure A. Match the figures at the dot, and hook them together with a brad. Turn the bottom wheel to read and study the memory verse.

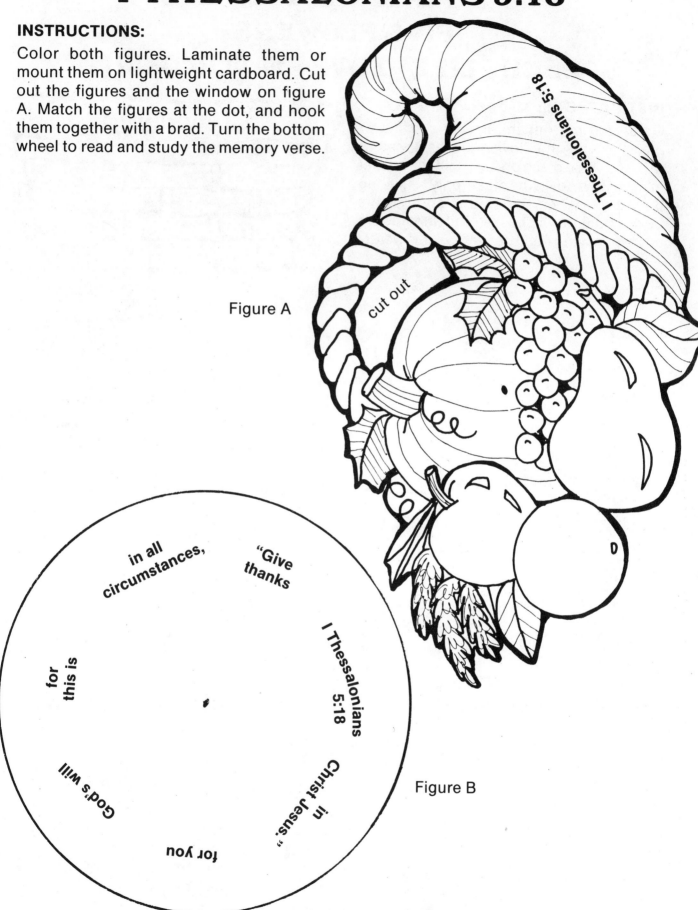

Figure A

Figure B

I Thessalonians 5:18

cut out

"Give thanks

in all circumstances,

for this is

I Thessalonians 5:18

God's will

in Christ Jesus."

for you

# I TIMOTHY 4:12
## FIVE FLOWERS
## SPEECH  LIFE  LOVE  FAITH  PURITY

**INSTRUCTIONS:**

Color and cut out the basket and flower pieces. Glue the flower pieces together with the verse piece on top. Fold the basket in half. Glue down the sides (only ¼″) along the edges. When the glue is dry, put the flower pot into the basket. Pull the flowers out when you need to review this verse.

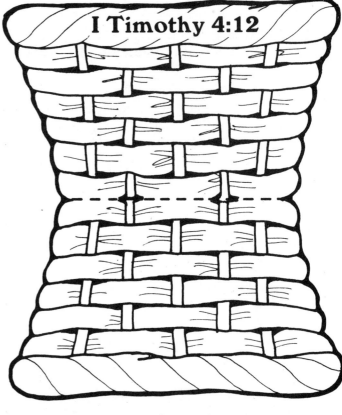

Figure B

cut out

Figure A

"Don't let anyone look down on you because you are young, but set an example for the believers in speech, in life, in love, in faith, and in purity."

SS1823

# II TIMOTHY 3:16

**INSTRUCTIONS:**

Color both figures. Laminate them or mount them on lightweight cardboard. Cut out the figures and the window on figure A. Match the figures at the dot, and hook them together with a brad. Turn the bottom wheel to read and study the memory verse.

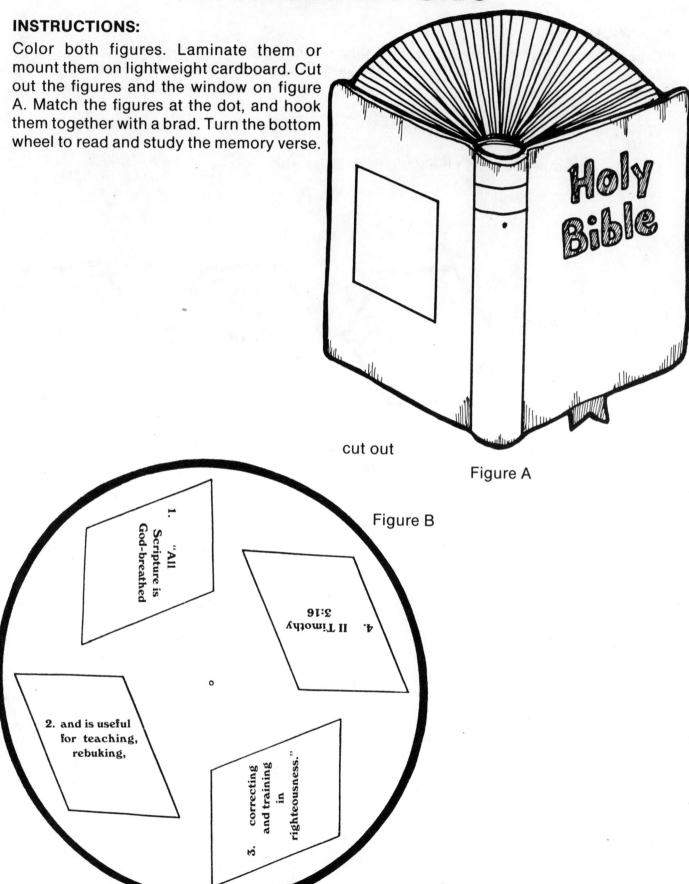

cut out

Figure A

Figure B

1. "All Scripture is God-breathed

4. II Timothy 3:16

2. and is useful for teaching, rebuking,

3. correcting and training in righteousness."

SS1823

# HEBREWS 13:5

**INSTRUCTIONS:**

Color and cut out the bee, the hive (found on page 85) and the puzzle pieces found below. Glue the bee and the hive to a 9" x 12" piece of construction paper. Glue the puzzle pieces onto the hive in order, so you can read and study this memory verse.

What does this memory verse tell us to "Bee"?

Can you find other verses in the Bible that tell us what God wants us to "Bee"?

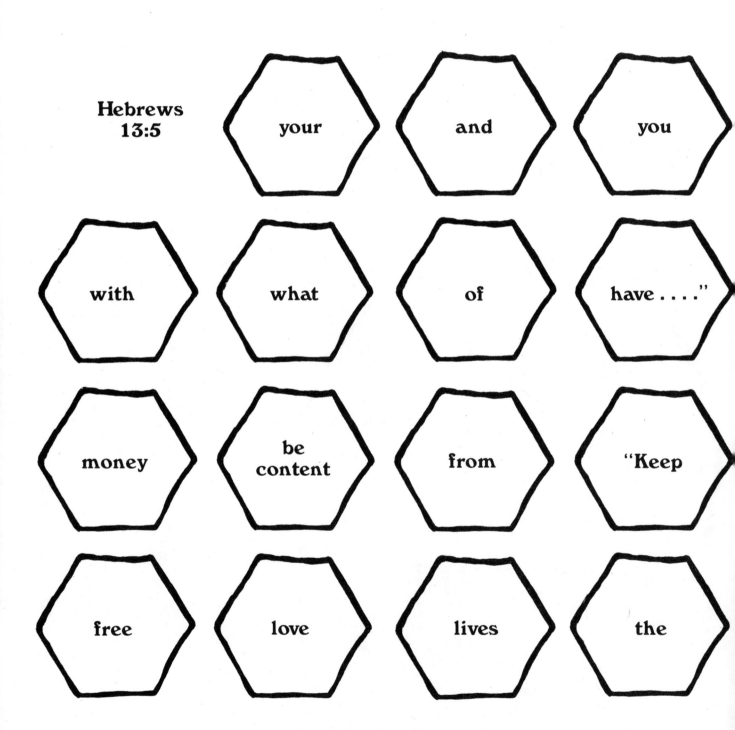

Hebrews 13:5

your

and

you

with

what

of

have . . . ."

money

be content

from

"Keep

free

love

lives

the

SS1823

# HEBREWS 13:5

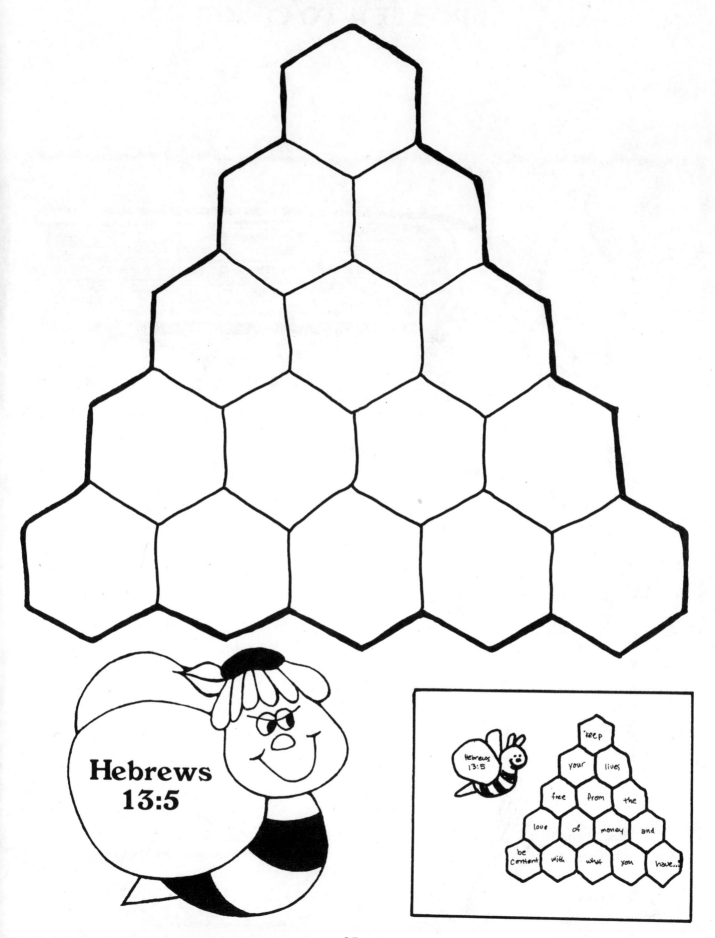

Hebrews
13:5

# JAMES 1:5
## A POSTER TO COLOR

SS1823

# I JOHN 3:18

**INSTRUCTIONS:**

Unscramble the words of this memory verse and use them as a caption on this bulletin board. Draw or cut out and glue pictures around the verse to show what this memory verse means to you. Display all of the small bulletin boards on a large bulletin board in the classroom.

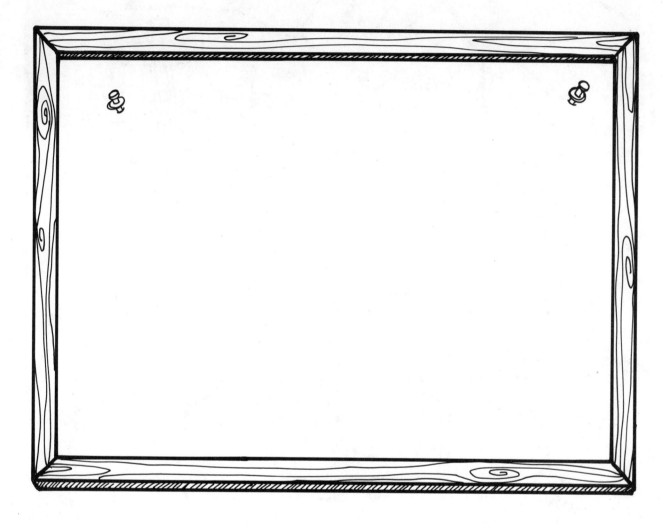

I John 3:18    with    words    in    with    or    us    love

tongue    truth."    actions    and    not    "...let    but

SS1823

# I JOHN 4:9

**INSTRUCTIONS:**
Color this memory verse poster. Mount it onto a 9" x 12" piece of construction paper to frame. Follow the trail to read and study this memory verse.

SS182

# A REVIEW ACTIVITY
## SCRIPTURE SCROLLS

**INSTRUCTIONS:**

Color the scrolls (found on pages 89-92). Cut out the instruction scroll and glue it to the front of a legal size 4⅛" x 9½" envelope. Laminate and cut out the envelope and all ten Scripture Scrolls. Cut each scroll in half on the black line. Review these verses by putting the scroll puzzles together. Store the review scrolls in the envelope.

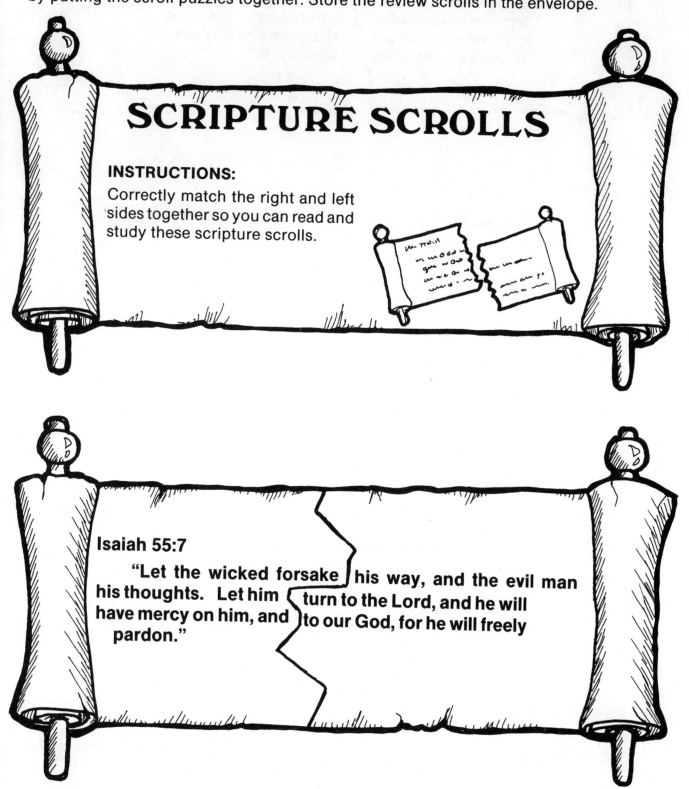

# SCRIPTURE SCROLLS

**INSTRUCTIONS:**

Correctly match the right and left sides together so you can read and study these scripture scrolls.

**Isaiah 55:7**

"Let the wicked forsake his way, and the evil man his thoughts. Let him turn to the Lord, and he will have mercy on him, and to our God, for he will freely pardon."

SS1823

# SCRIPTURE SCROLLS

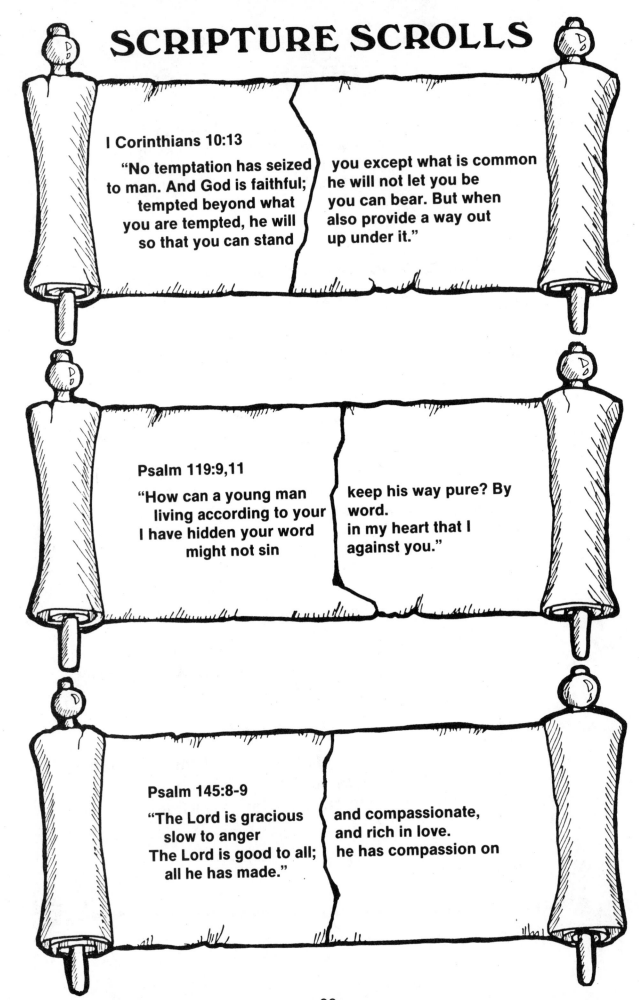

I Corinthians 10:13

"No temptation has seized you except what is common to man. And God is faithful; he will not let you be tempted beyond what you can bear. But when you are tempted, he will also provide a way out so that you can stand up under it."

Psalm 119:9,11

"How can a young man keep his way pure? By living according to your word. I have hidden your word in my heart that I might not sin against you."

Psalm 145:8-9

"The Lord is gracious and compassionate, slow to anger and rich in love. The Lord is good to all; he has compassion on all he has made."

SS182

# SCRIPTURE SCROLLS

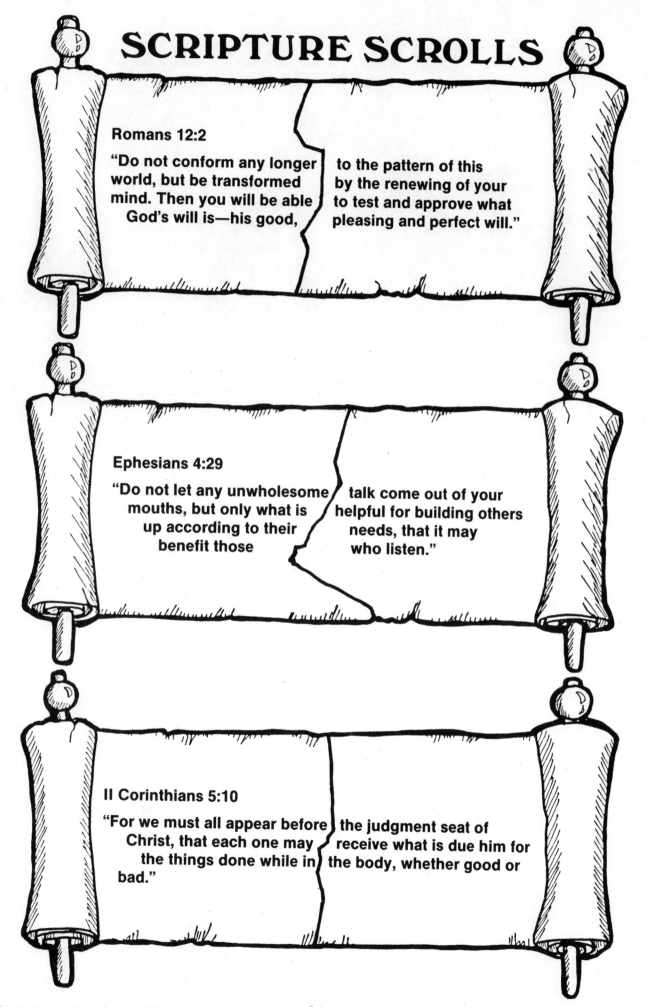

**Romans 12:2**

"Do not conform any longer | to the pattern of this
world, but be transformed | by the renewing of your
mind. Then you will be able | to test and approve what
God's will is—his good, | pleasing and perfect will."

**Ephesians 4:29**

"Do not let any unwholesome | talk come out of your
mouths, but only what is | helpful for building others
up according to their | needs, that it may
benefit those | who listen."

**II Corinthians 5:10**

"For we must all appear before | the judgment seat of
Christ, that each one may | receive what is due him for
the things done while in | the body, whether good or
bad."

SS1823

# SCRIPTURE SCROLLS

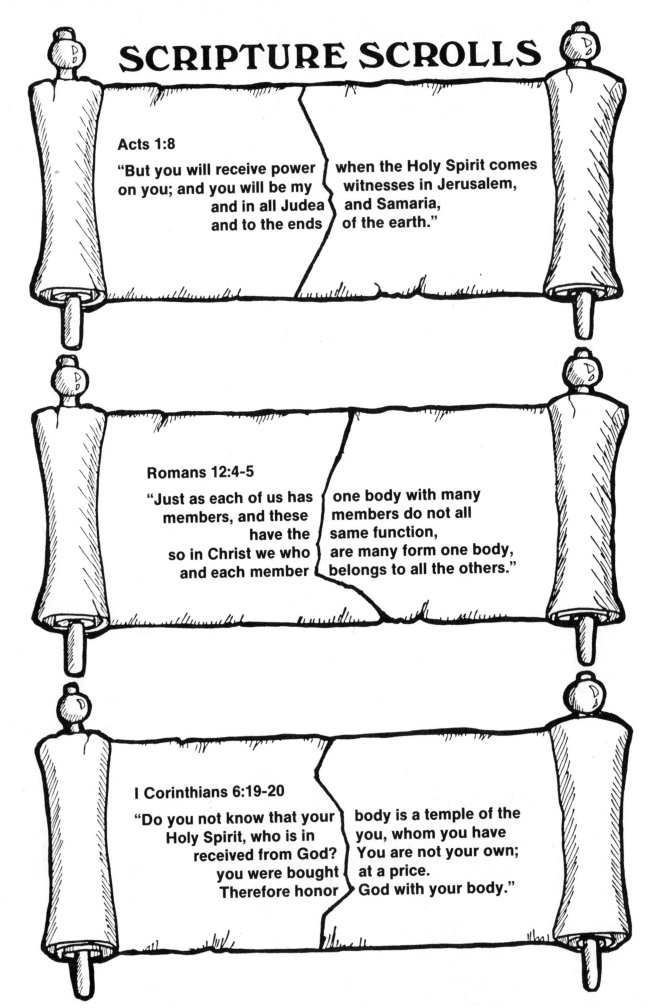

**Acts 1:8**

"But you will receive power | when the Holy Spirit comes
on you; and you will be my | witnesses in Jerusalem,
and in all Judea | and Samaria,
and to the ends | of the earth."

**Romans 12:4-5**

"Just as each of us has | one body with many
members, and these | members do not all
have the | same function,
so in Christ we who | are many form one body,
and each member | belongs to all the others."

**I Corinthians 6:19-20**

"Do you not know that your | body is a temple of the
Holy Spirit, who is in | you, whom you have
received from God? | You are not your own;
you were bought | at a price.
Therefore honor | God with your body."

SS1823

# A REVIEW ACTIVITY
## UNLOCK THE SCRIPTURES

**INSTRUCTIONS:**

Color the locks and the keys (see pages 94-96). Color and cut out the instruction card, below, and glue it to the front of a 9½″ x 6½″ envelope. Laminate and cut out the envelope and all the locks and keys. Punch a hole in the top of each key. You may wish to pin the locks to the bulletin board and have each student hang the correct key next to each lock. Or, use this as a matching activity at the table. Store the locks and keys in the envelope.

Instruction Card

# UNLOCK THE SCRIPTURES

**INSTRUCTIONS:**

See if you can unlock the Scriptures by matching the verses on the keys with the references on the locks. Check your Bible to see if you are correct.

Shining Star Publications, Copyright © 1990, A division of Good Apple, Inc.

SS1823

# UNLOCK THE SCRIPTURES

"For God did not call us to be impure, but to live a holy life."

"For it is by grace you have been saved, through faith—and this is not from yourselves, it is the gift of God."

"If we confess our sins, he is faithful and just and will forgive us our sins and purify us from all unrighteousness."

I Thessalonians 4:7

Ephesians 2:8

I John 1:9

SS182

# UNLOCK THE SCRIPTURES

"My help comes from the Lord, the Maker of heaven and earth."

"And my God will meet all your needs according to his glorious riches in Christ Jesus."

"...The Lord does not look at the things man looks at. Man looks at the outward appearance, but the Lord looks at the heart."

**Psalm 121:2**

**Philippians 4:19**

**I Samuel 16:7**

SS1823

# UNLOCK THE SCRIPTURES

"For all have sinned and fall short of the glory of God."

"Here is a trustworthy saying that deserves full acceptance: Christ Jesus came into the world to save sinners. . . ."

"But just as he who called you is holy, so be holy in all you do."

Romans 3:23

I Peter 1:15

I Timothy 1:15

SS1823